Co

Grubs and Bugs

3 cans (8 ounces each) refrigerated crescent roll dough
2 packages (16 ounces each) cocktail franks (about 60 franks)
1 bag (about 15 ounces) thin pretzel sticks
Alfalfa sprouts

1. Preheat oven to 375°F. Grease two baking sheets. Unroll dough; separate along perforated lines into 24 triangles. (Spray hands with nonstick cooking spray as necessary to prevent dough from sticking. Cut one piece of dough with serrated knife into three smaller triangles by cutting through widest corner. Repeat with nine additional pieces of dough. Slice remaining 14 pieces of dough in half.

2. For Grubs, place 1 cocktail frank on longest side of 1 large triangle; fold sides over ends of frank. Roll to opposite point, pinching dough as necessary to completely cover frank. Place seam side down on prepared baking sheet. Repeat with remaining large triangles. Bake 11 to 15 minutes or until deep golden brown. Immediately remove from baking sheet to wire rack.

3. For Bugs, place 1 cocktail frank on shortest side of 1 small triangle; roll to opposite point. With point facing down, poke 3 pretzel pieces into dough along each side to make legs. Place seam side down on prepared baking sheet. Repeat with remaining small triangles and franks. Bake 11 to 15 minutes or until deep golden brown. Immediately remove from baking sheet to wire rack. Place bugs on plate of alfalfa sprouts. *Makes 28 servings*

Night Crawler Veggie Rolls

¼ cup sesame oil
1 teaspoon freshly grated ginger
1 teaspoon minced garlic
2 cups snow peas, cut into matchstick-size pieces
2 large carrots, shredded
1 onion, cut into matchstick-size pieces
1 red bell pepper, cut into matchstick-size pieces
2 to 3 cups shredded Napa cabbage
2 cups bean sprouts
1 teaspoon salt
1 teaspoon black pepper
1 package (12 ounces) spring roll wrappers*
Sweet-and-sour sauce (optional)
Peanut sauce (optional)

**Rice paper spring roll wrappers can be found in Asian food sections of most supermarkets.*

1. Heat oil, ginger and garlic in wok or large skillet over medium heat. Add peas, carrots, onion and bell pepper; stir-fry 2 minutes. Add cabbage, bean sprouts, salt and black pepper; stir-fry 2 more minutes. Remove from heat and cool.
2. Dip spring roll wrappers in hot water until soft. Position wrapper with one point facing down. Place about 2 tablespoons vegetable mixture in narrow strip across lower half of wrapper. Fold bottom point up and over vegetables and tuck under filling. Roll packet up once to enclose filling securely. Fold sides in tightly, forming an envelope. Brush edges with additional hot water to seal; finish rolling.
3. For creature features, cut tiny eyes and mouths in wrappers and add additional vegetable strips for antennae. Repeat with remaining filling and wrappers. Cover with plastic wrap and refrigerate. Serve chilled with sweet-and-sour sauce and peanut sauce, if desired.

Makes 18 to 20 rolls

Night Crawler Veggie Rolls

Creepy Cobwebs

4 to 5 cups vegetable oil, divided
1 cup pancake mix
¾ cup plus 2 tablespoons milk
1 egg, beaten
½ cup powdered sugar
1 teaspoon ground cinnamon
½ teaspoon chili powder
Dipping Sauce (recipe follows)

1. Pour 1 inch of oil into large, heavy, deep skillet; heat to 350°F.
2. Combine pancake mix, milk, egg and 1 tablespoon oil in medium bowl. *Do not overmix.* Put 2 tablespoons batter into funnel or squeeze bottle; swirl into hot oil to form cobwebs. Cook over medium-high heat 1 to 2 minutes or until bubbles form. Using tongs and slotted spatula, gently turn and fry 1 minute or until brown. Drain on paper towels.
3. Repeat with remaining batter. If necessary, add more oil to maintain 1-inch depth, but heat oil to 350°F again before frying more batter.
4. Meanwhile, mix powdered sugar, cinnamon and chili powder in small bowl. Sprinkle over cobwebs. Serve warm with Dipping Sauce.

Makes 10 to 12 servings

Dipping Sauce

1 cup maple syrup
1 jalapeño pepper,* cored, seeded and minced

**Jalapeño peppers can sting and irritate the skin, so wear rubber gloves when handling peppers and do not touch your eyes.*

Combine syrup and jalapeño in small saucepan. Simmer 5 minutes or until syrup is heated through. Pour into heatproof bowl.

Makes 1 cup

Slimy Potato Bugs

1 cup pitted kalamata olives
1 cup packed fresh basil
¾ cup pine nuts or walnuts, toasted*
1 clove garlic
½ cup Parmesan cheese
½ cup olive oil
1 package (10 ounces) frozen potato gnocchi

**To toast nuts, spread in single layer on ungreased baking sheet. Bake in preheated* 350°F *oven* 8 *to* 10 *minutes or until brown, stirring occasionally.*

Combine olives, basil, pine nuts and garlic in food processor or blender container; process until smooth. Add cheese. With machine running, pour oil through feed tube, processing until well blended. Cook gnocchi according to package directions. Drain; toss with sauce. Garnish as desired. *Makes 4 to 6 servings*

Worm Cookies

1¾ cups all-purpose flour
¾ cup powdered sugar
¼ cup unsweetened cocoa powder
⅛ teaspoon salt
1 cup (2 sticks) butter, softened
1 teaspoon vanilla
1 tube white decorating frosting

1. Combine flour, sugar, cocoa and salt in medium bowl. Beat butter and vanilla in large bowl with electric mixer at medium speed until fluffy. Gradually beat in flour mixture until well combined. Cover and chill dough at least 30 minutes.

2. Preheat oven to 350°F. Form dough into 1½-inch balls. Roll balls gently to form 5- to 6-inch logs about ½ inch thick. Shape into worms 2 inches apart on ungreased cookie sheets. Bake 12 minutes or until set. Let stand on cookie sheets until cooled completely. Create eyes and stripes with white frosting. *Makes about 3 dozen cookies*

Potato Bugs

Cheesy Snails

1 package (about 12 ounces) refrigerated French bread dough
5 mozzarella string cheese sticks
1 egg
1 tablespoon whipping cream
2 tablespoons sesame seeds

1. Preheat oven to 350°F. Line baking sheets with parchment paper.
2. Roll out bread dough into 12×10-inch rectangle and cut in half lengthwise to make two 10×6-inch sheets. Cut each sheet into five 6×2-inch rectangles.
3. Slice each cheese stick in half lengthwise. Crimp piece of dough around each piece of cheese, leaving ¼ inch of cheese exposed at one end. Beginning with other end, roll into coil shape to make snail. Place on prepared baking sheets.
4. Beat egg and cream in small bowl. Brush dough coils with egg mixture and sprinkle with sesame seeds. Bake 20 to 25 minutes or until dough is browned and cheese oozes. Cool slightly before serving.

Makes 10 servings

TIP: Store leftovers at room temperature. To reheat, toast on lowest setting of toaster oven for 30 seconds.

Moth Cookies

2 cups sugar
1 cup (2 sticks) butter, softened
1 cup sour cream
1 teaspoon vanilla
2 eggs
4½ cups all-purpose flour
4 teaspoons baking powder
½ teaspoon baking soda
½ teaspoon salt
1 container (16 ounces) white frosting
Assorted food coloring
Assorted decors

1. Preheat oven to 350°F. Beat sugar and butter in large bowl with electric mixer at medium speed until creamy. Beat in sour cream and vanilla. Beat in eggs, one at a time, until light and fluffy.
2. Stir together flour, baking powder, baking soda and salt in separate large bowl. Gradually add to butter mixture, beating at low speed until well blended.
3. Roll out dough to ½-inch thickness on lightly floured surface. Cut dough using butterfly-shaped cookie cutter. Place onto ungreased cookie sheets. Use scraps of dough to roll into bodies. Top center of each moth with 1 rolled body.
4. Bake for 10 to 13 minutes or until set but not brown. Cool 1 minute on cookie sheets. Remove cookies to wire racks; cool completely. Frost and decorate as desired.

Makes 3 to 4 dozen cookies

Creepy Critters

½ cup olive oil
2 tablespoons red wine vinegar
2 tablespoons freshly squeezed lemon juice
½ teaspoon salt
1 teaspoon sugar
¼ teaspoon black pepper
⅓ cup chopped green olives with pimiento
2 green onions, thinly sliced
2 pounds fresh assorted vegetables (carrots, celery, asparagus, sugar snap peas, bell pepper)
2 cans (4¼ ounces each) chopped ripe black olives

1. Whisk together oil, vinegar, lemon juice, salt, sugar and pepper in medium bowl. Stir in green olives and green onions. Set aside.

2. Using crinkle cutter, cut carrots into long rippled shapes. Cut celery into thin slices and chill in ice water until they curl. Steam red bell pepper strips 2 to 3 minutes over boiling water. Curl to resemble wormy critters. Steam asparagus and sugar snap peas 2 to 3 minutes.

3. Place vegetables in large bowl. Pour marinade over vegetables; chill 30 minutes. To serve, spread chopped black olives on serving platter to resemble dirt. Drain vegetables and arrange over olives.

Makes 4 to 6 servings

Creepy Critters

Slimy Snails

8 ounces mostaccioli or penne rigate pasta
½ package (8 ounces) medium pasta shells*
2 packages (1½ ounces each) four-cheese sauce mix for pasta, prepared according to package directions
1 can (4¼ ounces) chopped ripe black olives
½ cup chopped fresh parsley
1 tablespoon paprika
¼ cup shredded carrots

**Cooked lasagna noodles can be rolled or coiled to form a snail as another option.*

1. Prepare pasta according to package directions. Reserve 8 mostaccioli noodles, 8 shells and ¼ cup cheese sauce to make snails. Layer remaining mostaccioli and shells with warm cheese sauce in 13×9-inch pan or serving dish. Sprinkle with black olives and parsley. Keep warm while assembling snails.

2. Sprinkle reserved shells with paprika. Assemble snails by placing 1 shell on top of each mostaccioli noodle, using a small amount of sauce inside shell to adhere. Insert 2 small shredded carrots at top of snails for antennae. Place on top of prepared dish. Serve warm.

Makes 8 servings

Crusty Crawlers

1 cup semisweet chocolate chips
1 cup peanut butter chips
3 cups crispy chow mein noodles
¾ cup toffee bits
18 maraschino cherries, quartered and well drained

1. Place chocolate and peanut butter chips in large saucepan over low heat; cook and stir until melted.

2. Remove saucepan from heat and add noodles. Stir gently with rubber spatula until completely coated. Spoon mounds onto waxed paper. Sprinkle with toffee bits, pressing down gently to adhere. Place two cherry pieces on each mound to form eyes. Allow to cool completely.

Makes 36 crawlers

TIP: Some toffee bits will fall between the mounds when crawlers are moved from wax paper to serving plate. Press crawlers onto the bits to adhere to the bottoms.

Fish Bait with Gator Heads

6 ounces assorted frozen clam strips, breaded fish pieces and breaded shrimp
1 cup tartar sauce
3 to 5 drops green food coloring
6 (6-inch) wooden skewers
6 dill pickles
2 pepperoni slices, cut into 3 strips each
6 to 8 pimiento-stuffed green olives
Mustard

1. Bake seafood pieces according to package directions.
2. Meanwhile, place tartar sauce in small serving bowl. Stir in food coloring until desired shade is reached; set aside.
3. When seafood pieces are cool enough to handle, thread 3 to 4 pieces onto each skewer. Place on serving platter and keep warm.
4. Cut horizontal slit in each pickle for alligator's mouth. Insert strip of pepperoni to make tongue. Slice olives to make eyes and nostrils; attach to pickle with small amount of mustard. Arrange alligators around fish skewers and serve with tartar sauce. *Makes 6 servings*

Fish Bait with Gator Heads

Caterpillar Chicken with Mushroom Ooze

1 package (about 17 ounces) frozen puff pastry sheets, thawed according to package directions
1 tablespoon vegetable oil
1 cup minced celery
½ cup minced onion
1 can (10¾ ounces) condensed cream of mushroom soup, undiluted
¾ cup milk
¼ teaspoon garlic salt
⅛ teaspoon white pepper
2 cups chopped cooked chicken breast
Fresh chives and/or black olives for decorating

1. Preheat oven to 400°F. Using round cookie cutter, cut each pastry sheet into 12 to 15 rounds. Place rounds on ungreased cookie sheet, overlapping to create 6 caterpillars.

2. Bake 17 to 20 minutes or until golden brown. Remove from cookie sheet; cool on wire rack. Use knife to remove top of circles and hollow out soft pastry underneath to make a "shell."

3. Heat oil in large skillet over medium heat. Add celery and onion; cook until tender. Add soup, milk, garlic salt and pepper. Bring to a boil; reduce heat to low. Cover and simmer 5 minutes. Add chicken and heat through. Spoon chicken mixture into puff pastry shells. Decorate with fresh chives and black olives, if desired.

Makes 6 servings

Caterpillar Chicken with Mushroom Ooze

Peanutty Halloween Cookies

- 1 cup (2 sticks) butter, softened
- ½ cup granulated sugar, plus additional for dipping
- ½ cup packed brown sugar
- ½ cup creamy peanut butter
- 1 egg
- 1 teaspoon vanilla
- 2½ cups all-purpose flour
- 1 teaspoon baking powder
- ¼ teaspoon salt
- ¾ cup red-skinned peanuts
- 1 container (16 ounces) prepared white frosting
- Orange food coloring
- Candy corn
- Red or black licorice strings

1. Preheat oven to 350°F. Beat butter, ½ cup granulated sugar and brown sugar in large bowl with electric mixer at medium speed until fluffy. Beat in peanut butter, egg and vanilla. Add flour, baking powder and salt; beat well. Stir in peanuts.
2. Shape tablespoonfuls of dough into balls. Place about 2 inches apart on ungreased cookie sheet. Dip bottom of glass into granulated sugar and use to flatten cookies to ¼-inch thickness.
3. Bake 12 to 15 minutes. Cool 5 minutes on cookie sheet. Remove to wire rack; cool completely.
4. Tint frosting with orange food coloring. Frost each cookie. Add 2 candy corn pieces for eyes. Cut small piece from licorice strings and press into frosting for mouth.

Makes 4 dozen cookies

Caramel Corn Apple-Os

7 cups popped butter-flavor microwave popcorn
2¼ cups apple-cinnamon cereal rings
½ cup chopped dried apples or apricots
¼ cup chopped nuts (optional)
1 package (14 ounces) soft caramels
2 tablespoons butter or margarine
1 to 2 tablespoons water
Long cinnamon sticks or wooden craft sticks (optional)

1. Combine popcorn, cereal, dried apples and nuts, if desired, in large bowl.
2. Place caramels, butter and water in large microwavable bowl. Microwave on HIGH 2½ to 3 minutes or until melted and smooth, stirring after each minute.
3. Pour caramel mixture over popcorn mixture; toss with buttered wooden spoon to coat. Let set until cool enough to handle.
4. Shape mixture into 8 balls with damp hands. Shape balls around cinnamon sticks, if desired. Place on lightly buttered waxed paper until ready to serve.

Makes 8 balls

TIP: These popcorn balls are best served within one day. Don't make them too far in advance.

Pumpkin Oatmeal Cookies

1 cup all-purpose flour
1 teaspoon ground cinnamon
½ teaspoon salt
½ teaspoon ground nutmeg
¼ teaspoon baking soda
1½ cups packed light brown sugar
½ cup (1 stick) butter, softened
1 egg
1 teaspoon vanilla
½ cup solid-pack pumpkin
2 cups uncooked old-fashioned oats
1 cup dried cranberries (optional)

1. Preheat oven to 350°F. Line cookie sheets with parchment paper. Sift flour, cinnamon, salt, nutmeg and baking soda into medium bowl.
2. Beat brown sugar and butter in large bowl with electric mixer at medium speed about 5 minutes or until light and fluffy. Beat in egg and vanilla. Add pumpkin; beat at low speed until blended. Beat in flour mixture just until blended. Add oats; mix well. Stir in cranberries, if desired.
3. Drop dough by rounded tablespoonfuls 2 inches apart onto prepared cookie sheets.
4. Bake 12 minutes or until golden brown. Cool 1 minute on cookie sheets. Remove to wire racks; cool completely.

Makes about 2 dozen cookies

Pumpkin Oatmeal Cookies

Meringue Bone Cookies

1½ cups sugar
Pinch of salt
5 egg whites at room temperature
Pinch of cream of tartar
1 teaspoon almond, vanilla, orange or lemon extract

1. Preheat oven to 220°F. Line 2 cookie sheets with parchment paper. Prepare pastry bag with round #10 tip (about ⅜-inch diameter).

2. Combine sugar and salt in small bowl. Beat egg whites and cream of tartar in large bowl with electric mixer at medium speed until soft peaks form. Gradually add sugar mixture, beating constantly. Beat until stiff peaks form and meringue is shiny and smooth. Add extract; beat just until blended.

3. Fill pastry bag with meringue. Pipe log 3 to 4 inches long. Pipe 2 balls on both ends of each log. Smooth any peaks with wet finger. Repeat with remaining meringue.

4. Bake 30 minutes; turn off heat. *Do not open oven door.* Leave cookies in oven overnight.

Makes about 2 dozen cookies

TIP: To give the bones an ivory or "aged" look, add 1 to 2 drops yellow food coloring with the flavored extract.

Meringue Bone Cookies

Candy Corn Cookies

Butter Cookie Dough (recipe follows)
Cookie Glaze (recipe follows)
Yellow and orange food colorings

1. Prepare Butter Cookie Dough. Preheat oven to 350°F.
2. Roll dough on floured surface to ¼-inch thickness. Cut out 3-inch candy corn shapes. Place cutouts on ungreased cookie sheets.
3. Bake 8 to 10 minutes or until edges are lightly browned. Remove to wire racks; cool completely. Prepare Cookie Glaze.
4. Place racks over waxed paper-lined baking sheets. Divide Cookie Glaze into thirds; place in separate small bowls. Tint one-third glaze yellow and one-third orange. Leave remaining glaze white. Spoon glazes over cookies to resemble candy corn as shown in photo. Let stand until glaze is set. *Makes about 2 dozen cookies*

Butter Cookie Dough

¾ cup butter, softened
¼ cup granulated sugar
¼ cup packed light brown sugar
1 egg yolk
1¾ cups all-purpose flour
¾ teaspoon baking powder
⅛ teaspoon salt

Combine butter, granulated sugar, brown sugar and egg yolk in medium bowl. Add remaining ingredients; mix well. Cover; refrigerate about 4 hours or until firm.

Cookie Glaze: Combine 4 cups powdered sugar and 4 tablespoons milk in medium bowl. Add 1 to 2 tablespoons more milk as needed to make medium-thick, pourable glaze.

Bat Cookies: Omit yellow and orange food colorings. Prepare recipe as directed using bat cookie cutter to cut out dough. Bake as directed. Color glaze with black food coloring. Decorate with glaze and assorted candies as shown in photo.

Candy Corn Cookies

Fish Biters

24 giant goldfish-shaped crackers
12 slices pepperoni, halved
12 Monterey Jack cheese cubes, halved
24 small black olive slices
24 flat leaf parsley leaves

1. Preheat oven to 425°F.
2. Coat baking sheet with nonstick cooking spray.
3. Place crackers on prepared baking sheet. Place 2 pepperoni halves on tail ends. Place cheese pieces on center of each fish.
4. Bake 3 minutes or until cheese is melted. Remove from oven and immediately top with olive slice to resemble eye.
5. Lift up olive slice slightly and place a parsley leaf behind it to resemble fin. Gently press down on olive to adhere. Serve warm.

Makes 24 crackers

TIP: Fish may be assembled up to 2 hours in advance. Complete steps 1, 2 and 3, then cover with a sheet of plastic wrap or foil and refrigerate until ready to bake.

Taffy Apple Cookies

¾ cup packed light brown sugar
½ cup (1 stick) butter, softened
½ cup chunky peanut butter
1 egg
1½ cups all-purpose flour
1 teaspoon baking soda
¼ teaspoon baking powder
¼ teaspoon salt
1½ cups butterscotch chips
1 cup dried apples
1 cup caramel apple dip
½ cup chopped peanuts

1. Preheat oven to 350°F.
2. Beat brown sugar, butter and peanut butter in large bowl with electric mixer at medium speed until smooth. Add egg; beat well. Add flour, baking soda, baking powder and salt; beat until well blended. Stir in butterscotch chips and dried apples.
3. Drop dough by rounded tablespoonfuls 2 inches apart onto ungreased cookie sheets. Bake 8 to 10 minutes or until edges are lightly browned. Cool cookies 2 minutes on cookie sheets. Remove to wire rack; cool completely.
4. Spread about 1 teaspoon caramel apple dip on each cookie. Sprinkle with chopped peanuts.

Makes about 4 dozen cookies

Alien Faces

½ cup (1 stick) butter, softened
¼ cup shortening
1 cup granulated sugar
2 eggs
2 tablespoons light corn syrup
1 teaspoon vanilla
½ teaspoon almond extract
⅛ teaspoon salt
2 cups all-purpose flour, divided
1 teaspoon baking powder
2½ cups sifted powdered sugar
⅓ cup whipping cream
Black decorating gel or black gumdrops

1. Beat butter, shortening and granulated sugar in large bowl with electric mixer at medium speed until creamy. Add eggs, corn syrup, vanilla, almond extract and salt; beat until fluffy. Add 1¾ cups flour and baking powder; blend well. Cover dough; refrigerate 2 to 3 hours.

2. Preheat oven to 375°F. Sprinkle flat surface with remaining flour and roll out dough to ¼-inch thickness. Cut out faces with oval shaped cookie cutters. Use edge of a teaspoon to form teardrop-shaped eyes. Place cookies on ungreased cookie sheet. Bake 8 to 10 minutes or until sides begin to brown slightly. Remove to wire rack positioned over sheet of waxed paper; cool completely.

3. To make glaze, sift powdered sugar and add whipping cream, 1 tablespoon at a time, until smooth and thin. Pour glaze over cooled cookies. (Waxed paper will catch drips.) Once glaze is set, decorate faces with black gel or use sliced black gumdrops to make eyes and mouths. *Makes about 3 dozen cookies*

Tiara Tarts

1 package (about 15 ounces) refrigerated pie dough
¼ cup sliced almonds
½ cup raspberry or strawberry fruit spread
¼ teaspoon grated orange peel
Powdered sugar (optional)

1. Preheat oven to 450°F.
2. Lightly coat 16 standard (2½-inch) muffin cups with nonstick cooking spray and set aside.
3. Cut out 16 circles from pie crust using 2½-inch biscuit cutter. Place 1 dough circle in each muffin cup, pressing gently to form ⅛-inch sides. Pierce in several places with fork and bake 7 minutes or until golden brown. Remove to wire rack; cool completely.
4. Meanwhile, arrange almonds in a single layer on a baking sheet. Bake 1 to 1½ minutes or until golden brown.
5. Place fruit spread and orange peel in small microwaveable bowl and heat on HIGH 15 seconds or until slightly melted. Stir with a fork until well blended.
6. Spoon about 1 teaspoon fruit spread on top of each tart. Top with vertical almond slices; cool completely. Sprinkle with powdered sugar just before serving, if desired.

Makes 16 tarts

TIP: Turn these tiaras into crowns by placing the almond slices all the way around the tarts.

Cheesy Pumpkin Biscuits

1 can (16 ounces) jumbo buttermilk biscuit dough
1 tablespoon butter, melted
1 cup (4 ounces) shredded Cheddar cheese
2 green onions, finely chopped

1. Preheat oven to 350°F. Separate dough into biscuits. Cut each biscuit into pumpkin shape using 3-inch pumpkin cookie cutter; discard scraps. (Flatten biscuits slightly to fit cookie cutter if necessary.)
2. Place biscuits on ungreased baking sheet. Lightly score tops of biscuits with paring knife to resemble lines on pumpkins. Brush with butter. Bake 9 minutes.
3. Meanwhile, combine cheese and green onions in small bowl. Split partially baked biscuits horizontally into halves with fork. (Biscuits do not need to be fully separated into two pieces.)
4. Sprinkle about 1 tablespoon cheese mixture on bottom half of each biscuit; replace biscuit tops. Bake 6 to 8 minutes or until biscuits are golden brown. Serve warm.

Makes 8 biscuits

Feet of Meat

2½ pounds ground beef
½ cup bread crumbs or oatmeal
½ cup milk or water
1 egg
1 envelope (1 ounce) dry onion soup mix
1 clove garlic, minced
8 Brazil nuts or almonds
2 tablespoons barbecue sauce or ketchup

1. Preheat oven to 350°F. Combine ground beef, bread crumbs, milk, egg, onion soup mix and garlic in large bowl; stir until well blended. Reserve 1 cup meat mixture.

2. Divide remaining meat mixture in half; shape each half into 7×4-inch oval. Place ovals on rimmed baking sheet. Divide reserved 1 cup meat mixture into 8 balls; place 4 balls at end of each oval to resemble toes. Press 1 nut into each toe to resemble toenails. Brush meat loaves with barbecue sauce; bake 1 hour or until meat thermometer registers 160°F. *Makes 8 to 10 servings*

TIP: When shaping feet, form "ankles" that have been "cut off" and fill with dripping ketchup before serving for an especially gruesome effect!

Foot of Meat

Backbones

4 (10-inch) flour tortillas
1 package (3½ ounces) soft cheese spread with herbs
1 bag (6 ounces) fresh baby spinach
8 ounces thinly sliced salami or ham
8 ounces thinly sliced Havarti or Swiss cheese
1 jar (7 ounces) roasted red bell peppers, drained and sliced into thin strips

1. Spread 1 tortilla with 2 to 3 tablespoons cheese all the way to edge. Layer evenly with one fourth of spinach, meat and cheese. Place red bell pepper strips down center. Tightly roll up; slice off and discard rounded ends. Repeat with remaining tortillas and filling ingredients.
2. Cut tortilla rolls into 1½-inch slices; secure with toothpicks. To serve, stack slices in twos or threes on serving plate.

Makes 18 servings

TIP: These would be great for a spooky breakfast! Use plain cream cheese and layers of fresh fruit. Try thin slices of strawberries and bananas for a sweet treat.

Anti-Vampire Garlic Bites

½ of 16-ounce package frozen phyllo dough, thawed to room temperature
¾ cup (1½ sticks) butter, melted
3 large heads garlic, separated into cloves, peeled
½ cup finely chopped walnuts
1 cup Italian-style bread crumbs

1. Preheat oven to 350°F. Remove phyllo from package; unroll and place on large sheet of waxed paper. Cut phyllo crosswise into 2-inch-wide strips. Cover phyllo with sheets of waxed paper and damp, clean kitchen towel to keep moist.
2. Lay 1 strip of phyllo at a time on flat surface and brush immediately with melted butter. Place 1 clove of garlic at 1 end. Sprinkle 1 teaspoon walnuts along length of strip.
3. Roll up garlic clove and walnuts in strip, tucking in side edges. Brush roll with butter. Roll in bread crumbs. Repeat with remaining ingredients.
4. Place on rack in shallow roasting pan. Bake 20 minutes.

Makes 24 to 27 appetizers

Anti-Vampire Garlic Bites

Snake Calzones

2 loaves (16 ounces each) frozen white bread dough, thawed
4 tablespoons mustard, divided
2 tablespoons sun-dried tomato pesto, divided
2 teaspoons Italian seasoning, divided
10 ounces thinly sliced ham, divided
10 ounces thinly sliced salami, divided
1½ cups (6 ounces) shredded provolone cheese, divided
1½ cups (6 ounces) shredded mozzarella cheese, divided
2 egg yolks, divided
2 teaspoons water, divided
Red and yellow liquid food coloring
Olive slices and bell pepper strips

1. Line 2 baking sheets with parchment paper. Roll out 1 loaf of dough into 24×6-inch rectangle on lightly floured surface. Spread 2 tablespoons mustard and 1 tablespoon pesto over dough, leaving 1-inch border; sprinkle with 1 teaspoon Italian seasoning.
2. Layer half of ham and salami over dough. Sprinkle ¾ cup of each cheese over meats. Brush edges of dough with water. Beginning at long side, tightly roll up dough. Pinch edges to seal. Transfer roll to prepared baking sheet, seam side down; shape into S-shaped snake or coiled snake (leave 1 end unattached to form head on coil). Repeat with remaining ingredients.
3. Combine 1 egg yolk, 1 teaspoon water and red food coloring in small bowl. Combine remaining egg yolk, remaining teaspoon water and yellow food coloring in another small bowl. Paint stripes, dots and zigzags over dough to make snakeskin pattern.
4. Let dough rise, uncovered, in warm place 30 minutes. (Let rise 40 minutes if using a coil shape.) Preheat oven to 375°F. Taper one end of each roll to form head and one end to form tail. Score tail end to form rattlers, if desired.
5. Bake snakes 25 to 30 minutes. Cool slightly. Attach olives for eyes and pepper strips for tongues with small amount of mustard. Slice and serve warm.

Makes 24 to 28 servings

Snake Calzones

Baked Brains

1 tablespoon butter
1 cup finely chopped mushrooms
1 jar (16 ounces) Alfredo pasta sauce
1 cup (4 ounces) shredded Parmesan cheese
3 eggs, beaten
3 sheets phyllo dough, thawed
2 tablespoons melted butter

1. Preheat oven to 350°F. Melt 1 tablespoon butter in medium saucepan over medium-high heat. Add mushrooms; cook and stir 3 minutes or until golden. Remove from heat. Whisk in pasta sauce, cheese and eggs. Set aside.
2. Fold each phyllo sheet lengthwise. Cut into 2 (6×8-inch) pieces. Fold each piece in half twice to form a 3×4-inch rectangle. Brush 6 standard (2½-inch) muffin cups with melted butter. Fit phyllo rectangles into muffin cups. Let excess phyllo hang over edges. Fill cups with mushroom filling. Brush edges of phyllo with additional melted butter. Gently fold and crumple phyllo toward center.
3. Bake 35 to 45 minutes or until knife inserted into center of cup comes out clean. Remove from oven; let cool 5 minutes. Arrange on serving plate; serve warm. *Makes 6 servings*

Abracadabra Hats

1 package (8 ounces) crescent roll dough
½ teaspoon dried basil
16 turkey pepperoni slices
3 to 4 salami sticks, cut into 2-inch pieces
2 cups pizza or marinara sauce

1. Preheat oven to 375°F.
2. Separate dough and place individual pieces on work surface. Gently shape each piece into long triangle. Sprinkle triangles evenly with basil.
3. Cut pepperoni slices into crescent shapes using small cookie cutter or knife. (Each slice will make 2 crescents). Place 1 salami stick piece along base of each dough triangle. Partially roll up dough to cover salami and create brim of hat. Place 2 pepperoni crescents on top part of each hat; place on ungreased nonstick baking sheet. Bake 12 minutes or until edges are golden brown.
4. Meanwhile, warm sauce in small saucepan over low heat. Serve hats with warm pizza sauce for dipping. *Makes 8 servings*

Mini Pickle Sea Monster Burgers

4 large hamburger buns
2 whole dill pickles
1 pound 90% lean ground beef
2 tablespoons steak sauce
Salt and black pepper
3 American cheese slices, cut into 4 squares each
Ketchup

1. Preheat broiler. Spray broiler rack and pan with nonstick cooking spray; set aside.
2. Cut 3 circles out of each bun half with 2-inch biscuit cutter. Set aside. Discard scraps.
3. Slice pickles lengthwise into thin slices. Using 12 largest slices, cut 4 to 5 slits on one end of each slice, about ½ inch deep; fan slightly to resemble fish tails. Set aside. Save remaining slices for another use.
4. Combine ground beef and steak sauce in medium bowl; mix until just blended. Shape meat into 12 (2½×¼-inch) patties. Place on broiler rack. Sprinkle with salt and pepper. Broil 4 inches from heat for 2 minutes. Turn patties and broil 2 minutes or until no longer pink in center. Remove from heat; top with cheese squares.
5. Arrange bun bottoms on serving platter; top with ketchup and pickle slices, making sure slices stick out at both ends. Place cheeseburgers on top of pickles; top with bun tops. Place drop of ketchup on uncut end of pickle to resemble eye.

Makes 12 mini burgers

Volcano of Doom

2 pounds sweet potatoes (about 4 medium), peeled and quartered
3 tablespoons milk
½ teaspoon salt
½ cup whipping cream
½ cup (2 ounces) shredded mozzarella and American cheese

1. Place potatoes in saucepan; cover with water. Cook 20 to 25 minutes or until tender; drain. Add milk and salt to potatoes; mash with potato masher until light and fluffy.
2. Spray pie plate with nonstick cooking spray. Mound potatoes in pie plate, forming mountain shape about 4 inches tall and 5 inches across at base. Leave 1-inch space between plate and potato mixture. Make deep hole in top of volcano.
3. Preheat oven to 350°F. Whip cream until soft peaks form; stir in cheese. Spoon whipped cream mixture into hole in volcano, allowing excess to run down sides. Bake about 20 minutes or until bubbling.

Makes 6 servings

TIP: Gravy from a jar could be added for effect as a moat around the bottom or dripped onto the sides.

Dragon Breath

2 packages (about 10 ounces each) refrigerated garlic breadstick dough
Minced garlic
1 to 2 tablespoons kosher salt
½ cup mayonnaise
3 tablespoons spicy yellow mustard
1 teaspoon dry mustard
1 teaspoon sugar
1 teaspoon lemon juice

1. Preheat oven to 375°F. Unroll dough onto ungreased baking sheet.
2. Roll 1 piece of breadstick dough for body of dragon between hands until dough stretches to approximately 12 inches in length. Place on baking sheet and twist bottom of dough under to form tail. Make small cut at top and bottom of stretched dough for mouth and tail using scissors or small knife. Flatten second piece of breadstick dough slightly and cut in half crosswise to form 2 rectangles. Make small cut on 1 side of rectangle for wing. Press edges of uncut side onto right side of dragon body. Repeat with second rectangle and place on left side of body. Repeat with remaining dough.
3. Sprinkle each dragon with garlic to taste and sprinkle evenly with kosher salt. Bake 13 to 18 minutes or until golden brown.
4. Meanwhile, combine mayonnaise, yellow mustard, dry mustard, sugar and lemon juice together in small bowl. Serve warm dragons with dip.

Makes 10 servings

Dragon Breath

Creamy Dreamy Taco Tomb Treats

¼ cup plus 2 tablespoons packed light brown sugar
2 egg whites
2 tablespoons butter, melted and slightly cooled
1 teaspoon vanilla
½ teaspoon ground cinnamon
¼ teaspoon ground nutmeg
½ cup pecans or walnuts, chopped
2 tablespoons all-purpose flour
2 cups vanilla or chocolate ice cream
Fresh chopped strawberries and pineapple
Chocolate sprinkles

1. Preheat oven to 375°F.
2. Beat brown sugar, egg whites, butter, vanilla, cinnamon and nutmeg in medium bowl with electric mixer at medium speed 1 minute.
3. Combine pecans and flour in food processor; pulse until coarsely ground. Add to sugar mixture and stir until well blended. Let stand 10 minutes to thicken.
4. Spray baking sheet with nonstick cooking spray. Spoon 2 tablespoons batter onto sheet. Using back of spoon, spread into 5-inch circle. Repeat with another 2 tablespoons batter, placed 4 to 5 inches apart. Bake 5 minutes or until light brown. Cool 1 minute on wire rack. Gently remove each cookie with metal spatula and place over rolling pin. Let cool 5 minutes. Repeat with remaining batter.
5. Fill each cookie with ⅓ cup ice cream. Wrap in plastic wrap; freeze until ready to serve. Top with fruit and chocolate sprinkles before serving.

Makes 6 treats

be the same

Meaty Bones

½ cup hickory smoked barbecue sauce
¼ cup grape jelly
2 tablespoons steak sauce
1 teaspoon grated orange peel
Nonstick cooking spray
12 chicken drumsticks, patted dry
Salt and pepper
12 pieces of gauze, 12 inches each

1. Preheat oven to 375°F.
2. Combine barbecue sauce, jelly, steak sauce and orange peel in small microwaveable bowl. Microwave on HIGH 1 minute or until jelly has melted. Stir to blend. Divide in half.
3. Coat wire rack and baking pan with cooking spray; arrange chicken pieces on rack. Sprinkle lightly with salt and pepper. Roast, turning frequently, 35 to 40 minutes or until no longer pink in center. Baste chicken with half of sauce; roast 5 minutes. Remove from oven. Dip in remaining sauce.
4. Let stand 5 minutes to cool slightly. Wrap bottom portion of each leg with a strip of gauze. *Makes 12 drumsticks*

Shrunken Dunkin' Skulls

Nonstick cooking spray
2 tablespoons cornmeal
1 package (about 14 ounces) refrigerated pizza crust dough
2 garlic cloves, halved
2 teaspoons dried basil
1 teaspoon dried oregano
2 tablespoons olive oil
2 tablespoons grated Parmesan cheese
1 cup marinara sauce, warmed
1 cup ranch dressing

1. Preheat oven to 400°F.
2. Coat baking sheet with cooking spray; sprinkle evenly with cornmeal. Set aside.
3. Unroll pizza dough onto cutting board. Rub with garlic and sprinkle evenly with basil and oregano.
4. Cut out 12 circles from dough using 2½-inch biscuit cutter. Place on baking sheet; stretch into oval shapes. Use leftover dough scraps to create eyes, noses and mouths.
5. Bake 10 minutes or until golden brown. Brush with olive oil and sprinkle with cheese. Serve with marinara sauce and ranch dressing.

Makes 12 skulls

Shrunken Dunkin' Skulls

Tombstones

¾ cup all-purpose flour
3 tablespoons powdered sugar
2 tablespoons unsweetened cocoa powder
¼ teaspoon salt
1 cup water
½ cup (1 stick) butter, cut into pieces
4 eggs
1 package (4-serving size) instant vanilla or white chocolate pudding and pie filling mix
¾ cup cold milk
Orange food coloring
1 container (8 ounces) frozen whipped topping, thawed
Icings and Halloween decors

1. Combine flour, sugar, cocoa and salt in small bowl. Bring water and butter to a boil in medium saucepan over high heat, stirring until butter is melted. Reduce heat to low; add flour mixture. Stir until mixture forms ball. Remove from heat. Add eggs, one at a time, beating after each addition until mixture is smooth.
2. Preheat oven to 375°F. Lightly grease cookie sheet. Spoon about ¼ cup dough onto prepared cookie sheet. With wet knife, form into tombstone shape, about 3½×2-inches. Repeat with remaining dough to form 10 tombstones, placing about 2 inches apart.
3. Bake 25 to 30 minutes or until puffed and dry on top. Remove to wire racks; cool completely.
4. Meanwhile, combine pudding mix and cold milk in medium bowl until smooth; stir in food coloring. Cover and refrigerate 20 minutes or until set. Stir whipped topping into pudding until well blended. Cover and refrigerate 20 minutes or until set.
5. With serrated knife, carefully cut each tombstone in half horizontally; remove soft interior, leaving hollow shell. Decorate top of each shell with icing and decors as desired. Just before serving, fill bottom shells evenly with pudding mixture; cover with top shells.

Makes 10 servings

Tombstones

R.I.P.
BOO!

Haunted House Cupcakes

1 package (about 19 ounces) brownie mix, plus ingredients to prepare mix
10 waffle ice cream bowls
1 container (16 ounces) chocolate or caramel frosting
20 graham crackers
Licorice pieces, chow mein noodles, candy corn, candy pumpkins and other assorted candies
Black decorating gel

1. Preheat oven to 350°F. Prepare brownie mix according to package directions. Place waffle bowls on baking sheet. Fill waffle bowls about two-thirds full of brownie batter. Bake 25 minutes or until toothpick inserted into centers comes out almost clean. Remove to wire rack; cool completely.
2. Spread frosting on cooled cupcakes. For each house, break 1 graham cracker into 4 rectangles. Press rectangles into center of cupcake vertically for walls. Cut another rectangle in half; attach to top with frosting for roof. Attach candies to roof with frosting for chimney. Decorate as desired with candies and decorating gel.

Makes 10 servings

Monster Eyes

1 container (8 ounces) cream cheese
6 miniature bagels, split and toasted
6 midget sweet pickles
Red decorating icing

1. Spread cream cheese evenly onto toasted bagels, leaving center holes in bagels unfrosted.
2. Cut pickles crosswise in half; insert, cut sides up, into bagel holes. Use icing to add "veins" and "pupils" to eyes. *Makes 12 servings*

Haunted House Cupcakes

Smashed Thumbsticks with Oily Dipping Sauce

Thumbsticks

1 package (about 11 ounces) refrigerated breadstick dough
12 sun-dried tomatoes, cut in half crosswise or 12 jumbo pitted ripe olives, halved lengthwise
2 tablespoons olive oil
Dried basil or dill weed

Dipping Sauce

½ cup olive oil
2 tablespoons balsamic vinegar
1 teaspoon dried basil
½ teaspoon salt
¼ teaspoon black pepper

1. Preheat oven to 375°F. Unroll breadstick dough; separate each strip and cut in half crosswise. Place on 2 ungreased baking sheets. Place tomato half about ⅛ inch from top of each strip and press down firmly; shape ends to round out tip of thumb.
2. Gently press down on dough with flat side of knife to resemble knuckles. Brush breadsticks with 2 tablespoons olive oil; sprinkle with basil. Bake 10 minutes or until light golden brown.
3. Meanwhile, combine dipping sauce ingredients in small bowl; whisk until well blended. Serve with Smashed Thumbsticks.

Makes 12 appetizers

Smashed Thumbsticks with Oily Dipping Sauce

Witch's Cauldron Pasta with Breadstick Broomsticks

1 pound corkscrew, cavatappi or rotini pasta
1 package (10 ounces) frozen chopped spinach, thawed and squeezed dry
1 package (3 ounces) cream cheese
½ teaspoon ground nutmeg
1 jar (16 ounces) Alfredo pasta sauce
Breadstick Broomsticks (recipe follows)

1. Cook pasta according to package directions.
2. Meanwhile, combine spinach, cream cheese and nutmeg in blender or food processor; blend until smooth. Combine spinach mixture and Alfredo sauce in medium saucepan over low heat; cook and stir until heated through.
3. Toss hot cooked pasta with sauce in large serving bowl until evenly coated. Serve with Breadstick Broomsticks.

Makes 4 to 6 servings

Breadstick Broomsticks

1 package (about 11 ounces) refrigerated breadstick dough

1. Preheat oven to 375°F. Unroll dough and divide along perforations. For each broomstick, shape breadstick into 8×1½-inch strip; twist one end for handle. Cut 5 or 6 slits (2 inches long) into opposite end; separate dough at slits for straw. Place about 2 inches apart on ungreased baking sheets.
2. Bake 15 to 18 minutes or until golden brown. *Makes 10 servings*

Witch's Cauldron Pasta with Breadstick Broomsticks

Yolkensteins

8 hard-cooked eggs
8 small tomato slices
8 wooden toothpicks
Mayonnaise
8 pimiento-stuffed olives
8 black peppercorns
Parsley
16 whole cloves

1. Cut thin slice from wide end of egg so it stands upright.
2. Slice egg horizontally, about ⅓ up from bottom.
3. Place tomato slice on bottom piece of egg. Reattach top piece of egg.
4. Use mayonnaise to attach slices of olives for eyes and peppercorn for nose. Attach parsley for hair and stick 1 whole clove on each side of egg under tomato slice for bolts.
5. Place mayonnaise into pastry bag fitted with writing tip. Pipe mayonnaise teeth on tomato slice just before serving. Repeat for all eggs.

Makes 8 servings

Serving Suggestion: Try serving these frightfully good treats to your kids for Halloween breakfast! Put out tiny plates of seasoned salt, sesame seeds, grated cheese and celery salt for dipping the eggs.

Yolkenstein

Lumberjack's Fingers

8 small sandwich rolls
4 frankfurters
Ketchup
1 radish
8 small sandwich rolls
4 frankfurters
Ketchup

1. Use handle of wooden spoon to push 2-inch long hole into end of each sandwich roll. Don't push all the way through the roll.
2. Slice each frankfurter in half crosswise, then cut notch in uncut end for "nail bed." Boil, steam or microwave frankfurters according to package directions.
3. Spoon a little ketchup into hole of each roll. Push piece of frankfurter into each hole, with notched end sticking out.
4. Cut 8 thin slices of radish and trim them into wedges. Place radish wedge on notched end of each frankfurter to make fingernails. Serve with additional ketchup for dipping. *Makes 4 to 8 servings*

Spooky French Silk Cream Tarts

½ cup sugar
½ cup unsweetened cocoa
⅓ cup all-purpose flour
¼ teaspoon salt
1¾ cups milk
⅔ cup semisweet chocolate chips
1 cup whipped topping
12 mini graham cracker crusts
Additional whipped topping
Small round black candies or mini chocolate chips for eyes and chocolate sprinkles for mouth

1. Whisk together sugar, cocoa, flour and salt in small saucepan. Gradually whisk in milk. Bring to a boil over medium-high heat. Cook until thickened, about 1 to 2 minutes, whisking constantly as custard can burn quickly. Remove from heat. Stir in chocolate chips until melted and smooth.
2. Pour custard into large bowl and cover with plastic wrap. Plastic wrap should touch surface of custard to prevent skin from forming. Refrigerate until cold.
3. Add whipped topping to custard and whisk just until combined. Spoon custard into crusts (about ¼ cup per crust). Cover tarts with plastic wrap touching custard and refrigerate at least 2 hours or overnight.
4. Before serving, form a ghost on top of tarts with dollops of whipped topping. Place candies on ghost to form eyes and mouths.

Makes 12 tarts

Voodoo Juice

1 cup water, divided
12 whole strawberries
24 fresh or frozen blueberries
12 mandarin orange sections
8 cups chilled fruit punch, apple cider or favorite soft drink

1. Place 1 tablespoon water in each of 12 mini (1¾-inch) muffin cups. Freeze 1 hour or until frozen solid.
2. Slice ¼-inch off pointed end of each strawberry. Arrange 2 blueberries at top of each cup of ice for eyes, 1 strawberry tip pointed up in center for nose and 1 orange section directly under strawberry tip for smile.
3. Spoon teaspoon of remaining water over each; freeze 2 hours or until frozen solid.
4. At serving time, remove ice by placing muffin pan in larger pan of cold water until faces release.
5. Pour chilled punch into small glasses. Place 1 frozen face in each glass. The water will gradually melt around the fruit, causing the faces to shrink and disappear!

Makes 12 servings

TIP: Frozen faces may be made up to 48 hours in advance.

Dripping Blood Punch

- 4 cups pineapple juice
- 1 cup orange juice
- 8 thick slices cucumber
- 2 cups ginger ale
- Ice
- 8 tablespoons grenadine syrup

1. Combine pineapple juice and orange juice in large pitcher. Refrigerate until ready to serve.

2. Cut cucumber slices into shape of vampire fangs (see photo). Stir ginger ale into chilled juice mixture. Fill glasses generously with ice. Pour punch over ice. Drizzle 1 tablespoon grenadine over top of each serving. Garnish each serving with cucumber vampire fangs.

Makes 8 servings

Mysterious Chocolate Mint Cooler

- 2 cups cold milk or half-and-half
- ¼ cup chocolate syrup
- 1 teaspoon peppermint extract
- Crushed ice
- Aerosol whipped topping
- Mint leaves

1. Combine milk, chocolate syrup and peppermint extract in small pitcher; stir until well blended.

2. Fill 2 glasses with crushed ice. Pour chocolate-mint mixture over ice. Top with whipped topping. Garnish with mint leaves.

Makes 2 servings

Dripping Blood Punch

Boo! Brew

4 cups cranberry-raspberry juice
2 cups white grape juice
8 whole cloves
1 small orange, sliced (with peel)
1 medium lemon, sliced (with peel)
Peppermint or multi-colored candy sticks (optional)

1. Bring cranberry-raspberry juice, white grape juice, cloves and fruit just to a boil in large saucepan. Reduce heat and simmer, uncovered, for 15 minutes.

2. Strain into pitcher or bowl, removing and discarding cloves and fruit. Ladle or pour into cups. Add peppermint or candy sticks, if desired.

Makes 5 cups

TIP: Brew can be kept warm in and served from a slow cooker, if desired. For more citrus flavor, remove mixture from heat and let stand 30 minutes, or make ahead and refrigerate until needed, reheating at serving time.

BOO!
BOO
BOO!

Sinister Slushies

4 bottles brightly colored sports drinks
4 to 8 ice cube trays

1. Pour each sports drink into separate ice cube tray; freeze overnight.
2. Just before serving, place each color ice cubes into separate large resealable food storage bags. Seal bags; crush cubes with rolling pin.
3. Layer different colors ice slush in clear glasses. Serve with straws, if desired.

Makes 4 to 6 servings

Trick-or-Treat Punch

Ingredients

Green food coloring
1 envelope (4 ounces) orange-flavored presweetened drink mix
1 can (12 ounces) frozen lemonade concentrate, thawed
1 bottle (2 liters) ginger ale*

Supplies

1 new plastic household glove

**For an adult party, substitute 2 bottles champagne for ginger ale, if desired.*

1. One day ahead, fill pitcher with 3 cups water; tint with green food coloring. Pour into glove; tightly secure top of glove with twist tie. Line baking sheet with paper towels; place glove on prepared baking sheet. Use inverted custard cup to elevate tied end of glove to prevent leaking. Freeze overnight.
2. When ready to serve, combine drink mix, lemonade concentrate and 4 cups water in punch bowl; stir until drink mix is dissolved and mixture is well blended. Stir in ginger ale.
3. Cut glove away from ice; float frozen hand in punch.

Makes 16 servings

Sinister Slushies

Putrid Bug Potion

3 cups lime sherbet
1 cup pineapple juice
1 package (.13-ounce) grape-flavor drink mix
2 cups ginger ale
Frozen seedless red grapes (optional)

1. Combine sherbet, juice and drink mix in blender container; blend until smooth.
2. Add ginger ale. Cover; blend just until combined.
3. Add frozen grapes, if desired. Serve immediately.

Makes 5 cups

TIP: Fake ice cubes with bugs or other critters can be added for an extra-buggy presentation. Make this grayish, ghoulish concoction pale pink by substituting cherry-flavor drink mix for the grape.

Putrid Bug Potion

Lime Chillers with Blood Drippings

¼ cup honey or corn syrup
12 drops red food coloring
4 cups chilled pineapple juice
6 ounces frozen limeade concentrate
3 cups chilled ginger ale

1. Combine honey and food coloring in shallow pan; mix until well blended. Dip rims of 10 wine goblets into mixture one at a time, coating rims. Turn upright and let stand to allow mixture to drip down sides, resembling blood. Place paper towel around base of glasses to catch drips.
2. Combine pineapple juice and limeade in punch bowl. Stir until limeade dissolves; stir in ginger ale. Fill each wine goblet with lime chiller.

Makes 10 servings

Note: This recipe can be doubled or tripled.

Hint: Instead of using ice that can water down the drinks, freeze seedless red grapes to keep chiller cold. Place single layer of grapes on baking sheet and freeze until frozen solid. Store in freezer in resealable plastic food storage bag until ready to serve.

Recipe Index

METRIC CONVERSION CHART

VOLUME MEASUREMENTS (dry)

1/8 teaspoon = 0.5 mL
1/4 teaspoon = 1 mL
1/2 teaspoon = 2 mL
3/4 teaspoon = 4 mL
1 teaspoon = 5 mL
1 tablespoon = 15 mL
2 tablespoons = 30 mL
1/4 cup = 60 mL
1/3 cup = 75 mL
1/2 cup = 125 mL
2/3 cup = 150 mL
3/4 cup = 175 mL
1 cup = 250 mL
2 cups = 1 pint = 500 mL
3 cups = 750 mL
4 cups = 1 quart = 1 L

VOLUME MEASUREMENTS (fluid)

1 fluid ounce (2 tablespoons) = 30 mL
4 fluid ounces (1/2 cup) = 125 mL
8 fluid ounces (1 cup) = 250 mL
12 fluid ounces (1 1/2 cups) = 375 mL
16 fluid ounces (2 cups) = 500 mL

WEIGHTS (mass)

1/2 ounce = 15 g
1 ounce = 30 g
3 ounces = 90 g
4 ounces = 120 g
8 ounces = 225 g
10 ounces = 285 g
12 ounces = 360 g
16 ounces = 1 pound = 450 g

DIMENSIONS

1/16 inch = 2 mm
1/8 inch = 3 mm
1/4 inch = 6 mm
1/2 inch = 1.5 cm
3/4 inch = 2 cm
1 inch = 2.5 cm

OVEN TEMPERATURES

250°F = 120°C
275°F = 140°C
300°F = 150°C
325°F = 160°C
350°F = 180°C
375°F = 190°C
400°F = 200°C
425°F = 220°C
450°F = 230°C

BAKING PAN SIZES

Utensil	Size in Inches/Quarts	Metric Volume	Size in Centimeters
Baking or Cake Pan (square or rectangular)	8×8×2	2 L	20×20×5
	9×9×2	2.5 L	23×23×5
	12×8×2	3 L	30×20×5
	13×9×2	3.5 L	33×23×5
Loaf Pan	8×4×3	1.5 L	20×10×7
	9×5×3	2 L	23×13×7
Round Layer Cake Pan	8×1½	1.2 L	20×4
	9×1½	1.5 L	23×4
Pie Plate	8×1¼	750 mL	20×3
	9×1¼	1 L	23×3
Baking Dish or Casserole	1 quart	1 L	—
	1½ quart	1.5 L	—
	2 quart	2 L	—